How To Live
with a Horse

How to Live with a Horse

By Frank B. Griffith
Illustrations by Rubye Griffith

Arco Publishing Company, Inc.
New York

Published by ARCO PUBLISHING COMPANY, Inc.
219 Park Avenue South, New York, N.Y. 10003

First ARCO Printing, 1975

Library of Congress Catalog Card Number 67-17383
ISBN 0-668-02783-5

Printed in the United States of America

To Our Best Friends
The Horses, God Bless 'Em

Contents

How To Live
with a Horse

1
The Nature of the Beast

OVER A PERIOD OF MANY YEARS WE HAVE RAISED, BROKEN, trained, ridden, and enjoyed horses. And we are ready to state, for the record, that it is great fun to live with a horse.

Sometimes it can also be dangerous.

That's why we have written this book. To pass along a few safety rules that will lessen the danger and heighten the fun.

The first and most important rule is to learn as quickly as possible the nature of the beast. Because your greatest safety lies in getting to understand horses; and this isn't as simple as it sounds.

For instance, contrary to popular opinion, a horse is not the docile, tractable creature he appears to be. And a horse is not a robot. A horse is a critter with a mind of his own and an overwhelming desire to please himself.

Also contrary to popular opinion, horses in real life and riders in real life do not behave the way horses and riders do on television, where a rider leaps on a horse and gallops off after the villain with abandon and flair. (Or so it seems.) Actually many television actors can't even mount a horse much less ride one, so a double or a stunt man does the riding and the actor merely sits on the horse in camera close-ups.

Before a rider can ride a horse with skill and safety many months must be spent training both rider and horse. It is not the purpose of this book to provide the rudiments of such training: advice of this sort may be obtained from books dealing with the subject of equitation or from a riding instructor. The purpose of this book is to acquaint the young or first-time horse owner with a safe means of handling, grooming, trailering, and enjoying horses. And, since this is best accomplished by understanding the nature of horses, we would like to differentiate further between certain facts and fancies regarding horses.

First it must be pointed out that no two horses are ever exactly alike. Each horse has a different personality; a different way of behaving; a different way of reacting to discipline and responding to affection. To handle a horse safely it is necessary to take time to fathom his individual disposition and temperament.

Many people who haven't owned horses will tell you that a horse is a remarkably intelligent animal, but this is true only of a fairly small percentage of horses. Many horses look intelligent but are actually stubborn or stupid, whereas other horses may not look too bright but may nevertheless prove to be loyal and obedient companions. A relatively low level of intelligence is easier to cope with in a horse than craftiness or cunning. In fact, a highly intelligent horse may prove extremely difficult to manage since the same ability that enables him to learn quickly also provides him with the means of outsmarting his rider.

The disposition of a horse frequently determines the

correct method of disciplining him. Some horses respond more readily when rewarded for obedience than when they are punished for disobedience. But with horses of more forceful disposition exactly the opposite may be true.

In any case when it is necessary to correct a horse because he has developed a bad habit that makes handling him or working around him unsafe, the correction should be immediate and humane; never coupled with a display of temper or brutality.

A horse is more apt to respond to love than to force. But even loving discipline should be administered with sufficient firmness to convince him that you mean business. A good guide in the matter of discipline is to treat a horse as you would a child: firmly, but with good will. A vacillating or half-way position merely confuses the animal at the same time that it encourages him to pit his will against yours.

In attempting to predict the behavior of a horse, it helps considerably to realize that the most erratic behavior in horses is caused by their deep-rooted fear of the unknown. A horse usually reacts to anything new, strange, or threatening by kicking at it or running away from it. When you understand this you can frequently anticipate a dangerous situation and avoid it.

But the author has learned, through long association with horses, that no one ever really knows all there is to know about a horse. Also, no two horsemen have ever been known to agree on the methods of handling, training, riding, or breaking horses. This is because a horse that is gentle and obedient most of the time is never gentle and obedient all of the time. And so those who are familiar with horses do not pretend to have the final answer to any problem of horsemanship.

One thing a first-time horse owner should know, however, is that a horse may act cantankerous now and then without being a mean or untrustworthy horse. A horse's moods vary just as the moods of a rider do. On certain days a horse may feel loving and tractable; other days he may feel jittery or stubborn. When this happens the thoughtful rider suspects that something may not be well with him. It will pay, at a time like this, to examine your horse carefully to determine the cause of his moodiness. If his unusual behavior persists you may want to have a vet look him over. Maybe his teeth hurt or he has a barley beard lodged in his jaw, or a stone may be stuck in his hoof. Possibly a saddle sore is developing, or an insect may be buzzing inside his ear. (Since a horse can hear sounds a mile away this could easily sound like a trip hammer inside his skull.) Or he may have stomach pains, or his kidneys may feel tender so that the saddle disturbs him. Perhaps the girth may be pinching him. Whatever the cause of his discomfort, for the sake of your own safety, you should investigate the cause of his ill manners and eliminate it before you ride him.

Many a horse has been given a bad name and even branded an outlaw simply because an undiscovered ailment was making him miserable. Instead of being condemned or sold, a horse in such condition should be given necessary attention, for if the ailment is corrected he may prove to be an excellent animal.

It is to be hoped that the facts revealed in the following pages will help the young or first-time horse owner to appreciate and to appraise a horse. But before going further the author would like to make one point which should never be forgotten by the reader who wishes to live *safely* with a horse. It is this:

ALL HORSES ARE UNPREDICTABLE!

ALL HORSES!

ALL!

2
"Let the Buyer Beware"

THOSE ROMANS WHO ORIGINATED THE EXPRESSION *CAVEAT EMPTOR*, "Let the Buyer Beware," must have had equine transactions in mind.

Unless you're an experienced horse trader you will want to be extremely wary when you purchase a horse. Because no matter how ethical the transaction appears to be, the buyer buys at his own risk. This doesn't necessarily mean that horse dealers are shady characters or that the seller deliberately sets out to defraud. It simply means that anyone can be fooled by a horse. And it also means that the perfect horse, like the perfect woman, must forever remain a myth.

Unless buying and selling horses is your regular business you're not apt to buy horses too frequently. In fact you may buy only one, and that's it. This makes the purchase of a horse very important to you. You hope to enjoy your horse for many years (and probably will if his age is as represented); you invest a considerable sum in the horse you buy (no good horse ever sells cheap, because of the vast amount of time and effort required to train him); and for you your horse will become a form of recreation; a hobby; a friend. No wonder, then, that you want very much to get a horse that will be just right for you.

If you get a suitable horse your experience with him will be richly rewarding. If you get the wrong horse, and by that we mean an improperly broken or misused horse, the results can be disappointing and even dangerous. Since this is so it seems like a good idea to consider some ways in which you can go about finding a well-behaved, manageable horse.

Horses are usually purchased in one of three ways:

From a friend.

From a breeder, dealer, stable, or riding school.

At a public horse auction.

If you've never purchased a horse before you should try, if at all possible, to buy your first horse from someone you know will be trustworthy. In this way you should be reasonably sure that the horse you buy will be as represented. However, it still makes good sense to ask that a veterinarian be allowed to check the horse's age, soundness, and general health. It is also correct to request a bill of sale legalizing the transaction.

If you are thoroughly familiar with horses and have bought and sold quite a few you may want to buy a horse from a stable, riding school, licensed dealer, or qualified breeder. A reputable dealer or breeder will consent to a vet check and will guarantee the horse to be sound, safe to ride, and in good health.

If there is anything wrong with the horse the owner should point out its flaws or its faults to the prospective buyer before money changes hands. Once this has been done the buyer accepts the horse "as is" and does not have any redress in the case of later dissatisfaction. A bill of sale should always be expected to legalize the transfer of a horse to its new owner.

If the horse (in this case a mare) is sold as "bred" a breeding certificate should accompany the bill of sale stating the date of breeding and the name and registration number of the sire, if registered. The new owner can arrange for the transfer of these papers to his name.

If the mare is purchased for the purpose of breeding and is sold as "open" — that is, not in foal — a vet's signature should verify the mare's condition.

If you have been raised around horses, understand them well, and know how to detect signs of poor conformation or lack of soundness, you may decide to buy a horse at public auction. However, since even the shrewdest horse dealers may sometimes be fooled by the appearance of a horse, this is not always the safest way for a neophyte to buy one.

A horse purchased at auction may sell at a lower price than one purchased from a private party or dealer, but the bargain can prove to be a costly one unless you are acquainted with the following facts:

An honest horse owner, selling a horse at auction, is supposed to tell the auctioneer of anything that may be wrong with it before the horse goes up for sale. The auctioneer is then supposed to relay this information to the assembled buyers. The horse is then sold "as is" and the buyer accepts it as represented.

Once the transfer of the animal to the new owner takes place the auctioneer is no longer responsible for the condition of the horse, nor is the original owner. In other words, the buyer is strictly on his own.

You can see from this that the auctioneer depends on the integrity of the seller regarding the condition of any horse being sold.

Unfortunately, however, not every horse owner is as honest as he should be and many times deceptions occur at auctions which make the purchase of a horse extremely risky. For instance, the owner may give the horse a tranquilizer — allegedly to keep it from becoming over nervous in transit, but actually to conceal the fact that it has a bad habit.

Or, a horse may be ridden in the auction arena by a rider skilled at highlighting its good points and minimizing its faults. In this case the horse may appear to be tractable but may prove completely unmanageable when transferred to different surroundings or ridden by an inexperienced rider.

Also, a horse may be trailered to a sale from a long distance and kept standing without rest or food for hours. As a result it may arrive at the auction block weary and dispirited. But the same horse may turn out to be a hothead when it is rested and fed and so may prove unsuitable for a beginner.

In addition to dispositional faults a horse may have physical deformities. Foot, leg, or hoof troubles may be concealed through use of illegal shots that deaden pain; or the use of special shoes having bars or padding may enable a crippled horse to appear sound.

A test should always be made of any horse purchased at auction to determine whether or not it is blind or deaf; and this should be done before the horse is removed from the premises — if possible before it goes up for sale. This is necessary because horses are sometimes offered for sale without reference being made to such conditions. Unless the condition of the horse's ears and eyes is checked before money changes hands, or before it is loaded for trailering, it is impossible to refuse the horse even though he may turn out to have faulty sight or hearing. Actually there

should be grounds for legal action if a horse that is deaf
or blind is sold as sound, but the unpleasantness and the
difficulties involved in such action could be avoided if the
purchaser would take precautions against defects of this
nature prior to the consummation of the sale.

And, as stated previously, the auctioneer is not liable
for any faults unless they are announced at the time of
the sale.

Difficulties involved in determining the precise age of
a horse introduce another factor which the buyer of a
horse must consider, whether the animal is purchased from
a friend, dealer, breeder, stable, or at auction.

As a horse matures, the cups of a horse's teeth change
and the slant of the forward teeth becomes more pro-
nounced. Unless you can look in a horse's mouth and
judge its age accurately, and this is very difficult to do at
an auction unless arrangements are made for prospective
buyers to examine the animals before they go up for sale,
you really have no way of knowing the horse's exact age.
Honest dealers will give you the facts. Others may attempt
to conceal a horse's age or at least to give and take a little.
It is possible for them to do this because after a horse is
ten or twelve years of age its teeth do not change noticeably.

The following poem, intended to be humorous, actually
provides a very sound means of verifying a horse's age by
examining his teeth:

TO TELL THE AGE OF HORSES

(AUTHOR UNKNOWN)

To tell the age of any horse,
Inspect the lower jaw, of course.
The sixth front tooth the tale will tell
And every doubt and fear dispel.
At three the middle "nippers" drop;

At four the second pair can't stop.
When five years old the third pair goes
And then a full new set he shows.
The deep black spots will pass from view
At six years from the middle two.
The second pair at seven years;
At eight the spot each "corner" clears.
From middle "nippers," upper jaw
At nine the black spots will withdraw.
The second pair at ten are white.
Eleven finds the "corners" light.
As time goes on, the horsemen know
The oval teeth three-sided grow.
They longer get, project before
Till twenty, when we know no more.

If you can have an experienced horseman or a vet check a horse's teeth before you buy the animal you will save yourself a lot of grief. But don't always imagine that a very young horse is the best to buy. For a beginning rider it is better to buy an older, more settled horse, at least ten years of age. It should be spirited enough to go along without constant prodding and at the same time gentle enough to be trusted not to take advantage of the rider's inexperience.

It is always a good idea to try to find out who owned a horse before you buy it and to learn, if possible, why it was sold. It may take some pretty deep delving to uncover the latter fact and you may never find out the entire truth; but if you are offered a good-looking, high-bred, well-behaved horse at a bargain price, you should make an attempt at learning what you can about its background because it is almost certain that it is up for sale because it has an undisclosed vice or a concealed unsoundness.

Horses that have belonged to children or been ridden in riding schools frequently develop bad habits (usually acquired in self defense against abuse or ·misuse.) Such horses have a tendency to take advantage of an inexperienced rider by stopping to eat along the roadside, turning around and heading back to the stable, or simply refusing to go on.

Horses that have been used in summer camps may be so run down by the end of the season that they do not show their bad habits until they are rested up and well-fed. Many are balky or stable sour (given to heading for home and hay the minute the reins are relaxed).

A horse owned by a woman may not behave properly when ridden by a man and vice versa. And a horse accustomed to a lightweight rider or a certain type of gear may object to a change of rider or tack.

Many people believe that a young rider should be started off with a pony because it will be more manageable or easier to mount. Frequently precisely the reverse is true. Many ponies are spoiled beyond reclaim because they have been treated as pets and not subjected to sufficient discipline to establish good manners. Others are so smart that they can easily outwit any unskilled rider. A gentle horse is safer than a clever pony for any young rider.

When the time comes to buy your first horse you should remember that the sex of the horse should always be considered before you make a final selection. A stallion, no matter how gentle he may seem to be, or how well-mannered his owner declares him to be, is not a suitable horse for an inexperienced rider. Even ·a gentle stallion may become excited and possibly unmanageable if he finds himself near a mare in season. And while in this condition he may injure his rider or bystanders

For this reason many riders prefer to own a mare. Especially since they may have the added pleasure of breeding her and raising a colt. However, mares can also be given to temperament. When in season mares may become high-strung and nervous, especially if they are ridden near a stallion. This can become a cause for embarrassment to young riders who ride in groups or who ride in shows.

Then too, if a mare is bred there will be a time toward the end of her pregnancy, when she should not be ridden. Nor should she be ridden immediately after foaling. When the colt is two or three months old the mare may be ridden "with colt at side," if this is practical. If the colt must be left at home, an inexperienced rider may find himself in trouble if the colt should whinny for the mare while she is still within hearing distance. Sometimes the most experienced rider finds it difficult to restrain a mare who is suddenly seized with a determination to rejoin her colt.

Considering the problems that arise in connection with stallions and mares, it is easy to see why the horse preferred by the majority of pleasure riders is a well-behaved gelding (emasculated male horse). A gelding is dependable and even-tempered and therefore ideally suited to those buying a first horse.

When you go to look at a horse with the intention of buying it you have every right to ask to see it lead in halter, bridled, and saddled; ridden at a walk, trot, canter (or lope); and loaded in a trailer.

You should observe the actions and attitudes of the horse carefully as it is being displayed to see if it takes the bit readily; if it allows itself to be saddled and girthed without kicking and if it permits the rider to mount and dismount comfortably.

You should also ask to see it back up since this is frequently an indication of the amount of training it has received. A horse that backs up without fighting the bit or attempting to rear is usually one that has received a fairly good amount of schooling.

Timothy Wright, fifteen, son of Mr. and Mrs. Clare Wright, of North Hollywood, California, with his gray western pleasure gelding, White Cloud.

Joanne Lindsley, fourteen, daughter of Mr. and Mrs. Charles Lindsley, of Cornell, California, with her prize-winning registered Appaloosa gelding, Mojave D.

If a horse lays its ears back, snaps at its owner when the girth is tightened, acts kicky around other horses, or runs up on the person leading it, it isn't apt to be a horse suitable for a beginning rider.

On the other hand, if the owner of the horse slaps it under the stomach, pulls its tail, or mounts it and slides off its rump, you may be reasonably sure that it is a horse safe for children to ride. If you are looking for a horse this gentle you should ask the owner to ride it without a bridle. If it guides with no more than a rope around its neck it is very likely well broken and suitable for a beginner.

If you snap your fingers close to its ears and it flicks its ears away from the sound you can be fairly certain there is nothing wrong with its hearing. If you move your hand back and forth slowly close to its eyes and it blinks or follows the movement of your hand, its eyesight is probably okay.

Even though you may not be able to judge its age by looking at its teeth, you should ask the owner to open its mouth so that you may see the condition of its teeth and its tongue. If a horse has a sore mouth, if its teeth are in noticeably poor condition, or if its tongue has been injured — which frequently happens because of the use of improper or cruel bits — you would only be asking for trouble if you were to buy such a horse.

After checking its mouth you should ask the owner to pick up all four feet. If the horse offers no resistance to this process he will probably be gentle to work around and easy to shoe. And while the owner is lifting his feet you should examine them to see what state they are in. If the horse is shod you will want to be sure he is not wearing corrective shoes, which might indicate that he has serious foot troubles.

If he is not shod you should make certain his feet are not so dry that the hoofs may crack. Also, the center portion of the hoof, known as the frog, should be visible and springy to the touch. And there should not be any trace of foul odor because such odor might indicate a condition called "thrush" which many horses get from standing in damp quarters and which may lead to serious hoof problems.

A horse with well-worn shoes has probably been ridden constantly, so you know that he is a worker. A horse with noticeable collar marks that is not a work horse has probably been driven in harness, and such a horse is frequently less flighty than one never broken to harness.

If you are an experienced rider you will want to ride the horse yourself before you buy it. But an experienced rider will not attempt to ride a strange horse until he sees the owner ride it and is able to form an opinion of its disposition and character. If the owner finds an excuse for not riding the horse the prospective purchaser may well be suspicious of the entire transaction. It is best to ride the horse initially in an enclosed area where you will have him more completely under your control. Having accustomed yourself to his gaits and mannerisms you should then ask to ride him away from the stable to see if he is stable sour.

If you are not sufficiently experienced to trust yourself to ride a strange horse, you should bring someone with you who is expert at judging horses and riding them and arrange to have that person appraise the horse and ride it for you. It will be best if the person chosen for this task is a trusted friend rather than a dealer, a friend of the horse's owner, or someone who might benefit financially from the sale.

Before concluding the transaction you should find out

if the horse you plan to buy has been worked in English or Western gear; if it has been trail ridden, used for roping, gymkhanas, barrel racing, or stock work. A horse may seem quite docile when ridden within the confines of corral or pasture, but when the same horse is removed to new quarters or exposed to situations which evoke memories from his past his behavior may surprise you. Horses used for cutting or roping can turn so quickly that they may unseat an inexperienced rider. Horses used for barrel racing may be reminded of their racing ability should another horse rush past them on the bridle trail and take off after it, again with disastrous results for the rider.

If a horse is sold as "green broke" it may mean that it has been broken to a halter or a hackamore but has not been trained to respond to a businesslike bit or taught to neck rein.

If a horse is sold as "well-broke" it should be familiar with several kinds of bits and gear; should neck rein, back up, figure eight, and respond to signals of heels and hands at various gaits. Naturally a horse this well-schooled will cost much more and be worth much more than a horse that is only partially broken. It will be a safer and more pleasurable ride and will prove an extremely rewarding investment.

In trying to decide the right price to pay for a horse the purchaser must consider the amount of time, skill, labor, love, feed, and other factors which determine its selling price. A good horse is never a cheap horse; conversely, a cheap horse is seldom a good horse.

Finally, if you would rather not own a horse that chews up stable partitions or fences, you should ask to see a horse's stall before you buy him to be sure that he isn't a cribber (compulsive nibbler).

And you should ask the owner to write down exactly what kind of feed the horse has been getting, the times and quantities of feeding, and the amount of water he is accustomed to drinking, so that you won't deviate too far from his customary feeding habits.

3

His Very Own Castle

IT FREQUENTLY SHOCKS FIRST-TIME HORSE OWNERS TO discover that owning what is known as a "pleasure" horse isn't entirely pure pleasure.

Unless you can afford stable help (and not too many horse owners can) you will find that every day, three hundred and sixty-five days a year (and add one more for Leap Year), you must feed your friend, water him, care for him, clean up after him; and — if you still have the time or the strength — you may also be able to ride him.

But before you earn this heady privilege there is something else that you're obliged to do: you must prepare a suitable home for him; and the time to do it is before you go shopping for him. We'll soon discuss the kind of home best suited to a horse's needs, but for the present there are other considerations that should be kept in mind.

If you live in a rural or semi-rural area where horses are welcome and there is plenty of room to stable and pasture them, it isn't likely that you'll have to face irate

28

neighbors just because you introduce a horse to the community. But if you live in a section where the zoning does not definitely state that horses are acceptable, there are certain things you should do before you buy a horse to avoid heartaches and headaches after you buy one.

First you should apply to the local zoning commission in writing for permission to stable a horse on your property. If they reply, in writing, that you may do so, keep the reply filed away for future reference. If they say you can't and their reasons seem valid and unshakeable, either do without the horse or move to a locality where horses are welcome. It would be pointless to try to keep a horse where they are not welcome. You would never really enjoy him, you could be forced to get rid of him, and you could lose some good friends in the bargain.

You should also check with the Board of Health regarding the following: Minimum amount of space required by law for stabling a horse; legal distance which stables must be from all living quarters (your own or a neighbor's). It is impossible to state these requirements because they vary from state to state and county to county throughout the country and are constantly being changed as rural areas disappear and new zoning laws are established.

In some states the Board of Health makes regular inspections of horse quarters in semi-rural areas to see that manure is properly treated against flies and removed from the premises at regular intervals. In other sections the ASPCA takes an active interest in the stabling of horses and makes its own inspections to be sure they are being properly cared for and not neglected or mistreated.

If you live close to neighbors, especially those who are not avid horse lovers, it is well to inform them in advance that you intend to buy a horse and that you will take proper sanitary measures to make certain that they will not be annoyed by stable smell, flies, whinnying, or stall-kicking. Many a friendship of long standing has been ruptured because of failure on the part of a horse owner to take this simple courtesy precaution.

It is a mysterious fact but nevertheless a true one that those who love horses are frequently not at all disturbed by the racy scent of manure that frequently surrounds them. Actually they seem to like it! Those not fond of horses, on the other hand, find the scent (?) of manure objectionable. It is a far less mysterious fact that manure accumulates quickly. The average horse produces about one large wheelbarrow-load per day. And those who find the scent of manure disquieting often consider the aroma of horse urine even more unpleasant. Therefore the considerate horse owner takes steps to keep these odors to an absolute minimum.

Horses when not kept scrupulously clean attract flies. And flies have a way of roaming. They're just as apt to visit the neighbors as they are to cluster around your home. It is because of annoyances of this nature that zoning is constantly being changed to eliminate horses, not only from suburban areas, but also from semi-rural areas — and if this continues horse lovers may find they have no place to stable a horse, much less ride one.

The considerate horse owner can do much to overcome this friction between those who admire horses and those who do not by taking the following steps to insure proper quartering of horses:

See that any stables or corrals erected for horses are located the correct legal distance from all human dwellings.

Remove horse droppings and urine-soaked bedding from stalls and corrals at least twice a day and dump in a pile out of sight and scent of neighbors, allowing for prevailing winds.

Dust the manure pile with about a quart of lime (slaked lime, not quick lime) at least once a day. This tends to sweeten the manure and discourage flies.

Arrange to have manure removed from the premises at least once a month if you live in a semi-rural or fairly well populated area. If you contact a local nursery they will usually remove the manure for you without charge. If you live in a rural area you will find a use for the manure yourself, mixed with straw, as a garden mulch or as a food for earthworms. But of course it will have to age to allow the heat to escape from it.

Having considered the comfort of your neighbors it is now important to consider the comfort of your horse. After all, his stable is his castle, and if you want him to be happy, contented, and cooperative, you should do what you can to see that his home is one he can be proud of.

If you were to imagine what it's like to be confined to a dreary one-room apartment 90 per cent of your time, an apartment without a courtyard, or even a view, you would have some idea of what it's like for a horse who is confined to a single stall, not big enough to lie down in and not big enough to move around in.

Just as your disposition would be improved if you lived in airy, spacious quarters with a garden or patio, so your horse's disposition improves when he lives in a double stall, properly ventilated, adjacent to a pleasant corral or paddock in which there is both a shady and a sunny area.

A horse loves to lie down and stretch out full length just as you do, occasionally. He also likes to be able to lie on his back and roll back and forth, from side to side, at least once a day. This may seem to be an idiosyncrasy but actually it serves a useful purpose. When a horse rolls in this fashion he not only relaxes and thoroughly enjoys himself, he also rubs dust into his coat which acts in much the same way that bath powder does for a human, absorbing excessive perspiration.

When a horse is fairly young he may roll back and forth several times, but as he grows older he may not be able to roll in one direction. This is why horsemen always say that each complete roll adds another hundred dollars to the price of the horse. They mean that it indicates a vigorous spirit and a supple body. Be this as it may, because horses love to roll and really feel deprived and underprivileged when they are denied this small pleasure, their living quarters should be large enough to permit them to engage in this little pastime.

Therefore, in designing living quarters for your horse, you should allow ample space for a double stall and a paddock or exercise area. If a horse's quarters are so small that he can't move around freely, he may suffer severely from the cold. But when a horse can move about freely he can stand even freezing temperatures without undue hardship.

But even in the South and Southwest, where the weather is relatively mild throughout most of the year, a covered shelter should be provided during the rainy season: although horses can stand dry cold fairly well, they do not do so well when exposed to damp weather.

Certain characteristics of horses must be considered in selecting the materials for stable and paddock. Horses given to cribbing (nibbling or chewing partitions and fences) will quickly ruin stables constructed of too soft wood. Also many horses develop habits of stall kicking or pawing that result in broken doors or partitions. Therefore only the most durable woods (of which oak is an example) should be used for stable areas, and all partitions should be nailed or, preferably, bolted together. If you attempt to economize in this matter and put a stable together with spit and baling wire you are apt to find it kicked to pieces or knocked down altogether in a very short time.

And once a stable is erected it should be kept in constant repair because if there is one exposed nail or split piece of wood, one rough spot or loose wire, you may be sure your horse will find it and get into trouble with it, possibly seriously injuring himself.

For the same reason stables and corrals or fencing should always be finished with lead-free paint; otherwise the horse may crib at the fence and swallow the paint, with unhappy consequences.

Windows should be provided in the stable wherever possible for sunlight and ventilation, but they should be closed against drafts at night or during inclement weather.

The floor of the stall should have clean, packed earth or heavy planking; but not cement, which remains too damp, slippery, and without proper drainage. The latter should always be provided so that urine will not accumulate in the stall. And, if affordable, floor surfaces should be covered with clean straw or shavings which should be removed regularly to avoid excessive dampness.

Since a horse may not be staked out, as a dog is — unless he has been trained from early colthood to avoid entanglement with a rope — it is absolutely necessary for you to have a fenced area for your horse, in addition to a suitable stall for him. The fencing should be firm, solid, and safe, NOT BARBED WIRE. Barbed wire may be used to turn cattle but it is unsuitable for horses, who may run through it if they become frightened or who may fail to see it in the dark. Also they may get their feet or legs tangled in it and become permanently disfigured because of a wire cut.

If you can't afford costly fencing and you do not wish to risk the danger of barbed wire, a simple and practical solution is to run an electrically charged wire around the pasture area. The installation is simple and the cost of operating is negligible. The wire is attached to metal posts about six feet apart, with porcelain insulators, and run to an electric fence charger. The fence charger gives a slight humming sound and usually has red and green lights which blink constantly to indicate that the fence is in operation. When only one light blinks it shows that a short has occurred on the line, possibly because a weed is touching it. Some fence chargers supply voltage which burns away the weed so that the line returns to normal without your having to seek out the source of the trouble.

A word of caution must be introduced at this point regarding the necessity for proper installation of an electrically charged fence since people have been known to be electrocuted simply because they made the mistake of hooking a fence charger up to house current. The only correct method is to have a licensed electrician do the job; then you know it will be installed properly.

If correctly installed the electric fence provides a humane but effective way of keeping your horse from straying. Once he hits his nose on the charged wire he will respect it and stay away from it. The charge is sufficient to reprimand him but not heavy enough to harm him. Nor will it harm anyone who touches the wire by accident. You may leap into the air in surprise on first contact, but there is really no danger involved — provided, as stated above, that the line is professionally installed.

Out of courtesy to visitors it is a good idea to hang a sign somewhere stating that the fence is electrically charged. And children — your own or a neighbor's — should be warned not to touch the fence at any time. When you are showing your horse off to guests or you must go back and forth through it to feed him or otherwise attend to him, simply disconnect the line temporarily.

If you live near a public highway you must take special care to see that your horse is properly fenced because if he should get out on the road and cause personal or property damage you would be held completely liable for such damage; and this would not be a good way to encourage public acceptance of horses in your locality.

A discussion of suitable living quarters for your horse would not be complete if it did not include suggestions for proper home furnishings and so, in this connection, we'd like to point out some of the things he will need in both stall and paddock to insure his comfort.

A horse should have a firmly anchored manger or feed box or feeding rack in one corner of his stall from which he may eat hay or grain.

We will also need an automatic drinker or a receptacle that will hold water. A pail set in the paddock or stall is not a satisfactory means of providing water for a horse because he will invariably upset the pail the moment your back is turned and be left without water for too long a period.

If you must use a pail or bucket for water, attach it firmly to a stall partition or fence section at a height which makes it impossible for him to put his foot in it. (Something horses love to do.)

Doors to stalls should open freely to allow safe entry and egress for both horse and owner and they should lock with a latch which a horse cannot learn to open easily. (Some horses are very adept at this and also quite gifted at untying ropes.)

A stallion or a horse that bites should have a grille or ladder hung across the upper part of the stall so that he cannot nip at people or other horses. And a grille partition should separate individual stalls for the same reason.

Stable roofs should be made leakproof for obvious reasons. And, if at all possible, arrangements should be made to light the stable area, since horses frequently require attention at night.

4
Yours, All Yours

WHEN HIS BILL OF SALE IS IN YOUR POCKET AND HIS PRESENCE on your property tells you that you own him, you are ready to live with a horse.

If it is your first horse you will scarcely be able to stand the proud tingle of ownership. Now at last he is yours, all yours. The prospect of adventures together is heady with excitement. You see yourself galloping gracefully across sun-dappled meadows; trotting soberly down shaded lanes. . . . All this is for the future.

For the present you must learn how to be groom, nursemaid, friend, and analyst to an animal who for all his velvet-eyed beauty and sleekness of limb would just as soon kick you as look at you. If you have never owned a horse before this bald statement of truth will amaze or even offend you. You are confident that because you love your horse and express your love for him, he will quite naturally love you back.

Such is not the case.

Horses that are gentle by nature remain gentle most of

the time and do not deliberately set out to injure their owners. But the horse that actively, faithfully, and unvaryingly returns his owner's love is rare indeed. If you should find yourself in possession of such a horse, treasure him. But don't imagine for an instant that the horse you purchased is such a horse till you have had time to study him, observe his habits, and fathom his disposition.

To help you do this the soundest advice we can offer you if you have just bought your first horse is: TAKE TIME TO GET ACQUAINTED WITH ANY HORSE BEFORE YOU RIDE HIM. First do whatever needs to be done to put him in good condition. This may mean having him wormed or giving him a supplementary vitamin feed; or having a vet look him over. (If this wasn't done before you bought him.)

Next have his feet attended to. If his shoes look as if they've been worn a long time you may want to have him completely re-shod. Or the blacksmith may decide that the shoes merely need to be re-set. If he is without shoes and you can't afford to have him shod right away you will at least want to have his hooves trimmed.

At this point it seems advisable to dwell for a moment on the subject of horseshoeing and farriers. (Blacksmiths or horseshoers.)

If a horse is to be ridden frequently on hard roads he should be shod. If he is to be turned out with other horses you may want to have only his front feet shod so that he won't seriously injure another horse if he proves kicky. But if he is to be kept up or kept by himself he should have all four feet shod.

Under average use and following a normal pattern of growth a horse usually needs to be shod every four to six weeks. Some horses' hooves grow faster or slower and the period between shoeings may be shortened or lengthened accordingly.

Skillful shoeing is an art not known to every blacksmith. Some are considerably more expert than others. The best way to find a reliable blacksmith is to seek out someone who owns horses and has had them shod with the same smith over a period of time. You can usually trust the recommendation of such a person.

If you really don't know anything about the shoeing of a horse you shouldn't tell the blacksmith what to do; leave things to his own good judgement. But you should quickly find out as much as you can about proper shoeing of your particular kind of horse because correct shoeing can help to keep your horse comfortable and more responsive to your demands, whereas improper shoeing may cause lameness in a horse and could lead to even more serious foot or leg troubles which might render him useless for riding.

Before a blacksmith attempts to shoe a horse he should be told how you intend to use him. Roping, barrel racing, pleasure riding, jumping, and show riding call for specialized kinds of shoeing and a skilled blacksmith selects just the right shoe for your needs.

Cold shoeing, the use of standard shoes which are not fired and shaped to the individual horse's hooves, are not recommended unless you cannot find a blacksmith capable of forging custom-made shoes; or unless you can't afford the cost of fired shoes. It is well worth your while to pay the additional cost of specially fitted, fired shoes and to hire the services of a capable blacksmith if you hope to enjoy riding your horse and have him enjoy your good times together.

As you become better acquainted with the gaits and specific foot problems of your horse, you will discover that highly specialized or corrective shoeing can overcome faulty gaits in a horse and add greatly to his style and smoothness.

Never allow shoes to remain on your horse past the period recommended by the blacksmith; otherwise, besides becoming painful and unwieldy, they could cause a condition known as contracted hoof, which might lower the value of your horse or even make it impossible for you to ride him.

If you find that you can't always afford to have shoes replaced within the proper length of time, you should have the shoes "pulled" (that is, removed from the horse's feet) so they won't cause discomfort or injury. And if a shoe should come loose or if a horse pulls his shoe while you are riding him or when he is out in pasture, you should have the blacksmith replace or adjust the shoe as quickly as possible.

In hiring the services of a new blacksmith you should try to arrange to be present while the horse is being shod, not only to see that the shoeing is being done properly, but also to see that the blacksmith handles the horse in an understanding manner. If a blacksmith mistreats the horse, causing the animal to pull back or otherwise misbehave, or if he flails at the horse in an effort to control him, possibly causing him to become head-shy, you will certainly not want such a blacksmith to shoe your horse again.

After a horse's feet have been cared for the new owner should next ask a vet to see if his teeth need attention. The teeth of the average horse are all too frequently neglected, causing him to suffer pain when a bit is inserted in his mouth or when he attempts to chew his food. Sometimes his teeth develop rough, sharp edges which cut into his cheeks. This prevents proper chewing, makes it difficult for him to digest his food, and may cause him to look run down or "poor." (If a horse's flanks cave in horsemen say he is "g'anted." This may be caused by neglected teeth, though it could mean he lacks sufficient feed or water.)

If you ask the vet to "float his teeth," you will be asking him to smooth away any rough edges and to line up his bite. This should be done before you increase his rations in an effort to improve his appearance because this one simple measure may enable him to digest his food better and so he will look well without necessarily increasing his feed. For full details on feeding, see Chapter 5.

Any horse may appear to be nervous or ill at ease for several days after being moved to new quarters. Every sight, sound, and smell is unfamiliar to him; even the manner of feeding and watering, saddling and bridling, may be different from what he's been accustomed to. If he has been separated from horses he was fond of and taken to a place where there are no horses he will be especially restive because horses are herd animals and feel most secure when surrounded by their own kind.

When you become aware of the many factors which can disturb your horse in new surroundings, you will be more patient with him and you certainly should not attempt to judge either his character or his disposition for several days after you introduce him to his new quarters.

Many horses experience such great fear at being transported to new surroundings that they develop distemper. Since this disease is considered highly contagious among horses and frequently proves fatal, you should put any new horse in quarantine if he has been purchased at auction or shipped from another state. Some owners arrange for any new horse to be given a distemper shot. In either case the veterinarian should decide when it is permissible to allow it around other horses. The horse in quarantine should be provided with a separate stall and bedding, removed from other horses and should be fed and watered from separate properly disinfected containers and allotted separate tack and grooming implements, including feed boxes and watering tubs, blankets, etc. His droppings should be removed separately and buried, and when the vet gives him a clean bill of health the stall and all equipment should be sterilized.

A new horse should be allowed to rest. He should be watered generously (even though he may not drink for a while because of the change in water) and he should be introduced to new feed or new feeding habits gradually.

Since a horse may have been accustomed to a feeding method which you cannot duplicate you should observe his droppings to make certain that they are firm and moist, not loose or hard. In this way you will be able to *tell* whether or not his new feed is agreeing with him.

An inexperienced rider should not attempt to bridle, saddle, or ride a newly purchased horse until an experienced rider rides him for a sufficient length of time to be able to tell if he has any dangerous habits.

A horse knows by the way a rider mounts and conveys signals whether the rider is fearful or confident, experienced or a novice, and the horse will react accordingly. If you doubt this, watch the same horse ridden by a beginner and then by an experienced horseman; the difference in his behavior will amaze you.

When you have reached a point where you feel that you are ready to ride your new horse yourself, that is, when you feel confident that he doesn't have any serious vices, you are ready to find just the right saddle and bridle for him as well as any other gear that may be required in riding him. The proper selection of his gear and other appurtenances will be discussed in detail in Chapter 6.

5
Feeding the Brute

A HORSE IS FED HAY AND GRAIN, OR OTHER SUPPLEMENTARY feeds, in quantities determined by his body weight and build and the amount and kind of work that is required of him.

Clean, fresh water should be available to him at all times but he should not be allowed to drink water if he is over-heated or over-tired from strenuous exertion.

Automatic drinkers which regulate the flow of water are of course the most convenient method of watering but not too many amateur horse owners can afford them. If another receptacle is provided which must be filled by bucket or hose the receptacle should be emptied and thoroughly cleaned frequently and inspected at least once a day. Inspection is necessary because leaves, insects, bits of hay and grain, birds, or other small animals may fall into the water and contaminate it. A horse that is worked regularly, and by this we mean a minimum of two or three hours a day, should receive grain in addition to hay. A horse that stands idle for days at a time should not be fed grain because he may become too spirited for a beginning rider to handle safely.

Some horse owners feed hay in pellet form, especially when trailering horses to shows or on trail rides away from home. This type of feed is handy and practical for this purpose because it is less bulky than hay and contains everything a horse is known to need for proper nourishment.

Under average working conditions a horse will usually stay in good condition if he is fed two flakes of hay — that is, two sections of the bale — in the morning, and two flakes at night, plus all the water he will drink. (This assumes that the hay is in 80-pound bales.)

If you plan to work a horse strenuously you should increase his hay ration or add grain or a special conditioning feed, the exact amount to be determined after consultation with your veterinarian.

If you feed baled hay you should keep a pair of cutting pliers and a set of hay hooks near the hay. You will need the hay hooks as an aid in handling the bales and the pliers for removing the baling wire. The hay hooks should always be hung out of the reach of children with the hooks tucked into the hay, and the baling wire should be folded and the ends wrapped securely around the middle as the wires are removed from each bale. Arrangements should be made to dispose of baling wire and if it is impossible to do this oftener than once a month, the wire should be stored in a closed container while waiting for rubbish collection.

Hay should always be stored where it will be sheltered from rain or snow because if hay becomes damp and then dries out while it is baled it may become mouldy, and mouldy hay is not good for horses since it may cause serious digestive disturbances. A good plan is to shake all hay out before feeding it so that you can detect any mouldy portions and discard them.

If you can't afford a hay barn or specially constructed shelter you should cover your hay with waterproof tarpaulins tied down and anchored against the wind.

Hay should be fed from a hay rack or similar dispenser which allows the horse to eat it without taking in sand or dirt, which might result in colic. And the same holds true for grain. Horses should never be fed from the ground except in grassy pasture because they will take in unhealthy amounts of dirt with the feeding. And hay and grain should be inspected for foreign matter before feeding because stones, twigs, nails, or other objects, if left undetected, also could cause injury.

It is best to store grain in metal-covered containers whenever possible so that rodents won't get into it.

And in feeding a horse, whether hay or grain, it is well to keep these safety rules in mind:

Even the gentlest horse may become excited at feeding time and rather unmanageable, so it's wise to take the precaution of keeping him tied till you have placed his feed in manger or hay rack. In this way you will know that he can't paw at you or kick at you in his eagerness to start eating.

If you must lead a horse to feed you shouldn't attempt to do so simply by throwing a lead rope around his neck. A better plan is to put a halter on him and attach the lead rope to that; or fasten the tie rope around his neck and twist a portion of it around his nose. This is called "snubbing" him, a term which has nothing to do with social status. It is simply a means of establishing better control over a skittery horse.

One point that should be covered in connection with

feeding concerns a belief common to many horse owners: that a horse is sure to love his owner more if the owner feeds him tidbits as a sign of affection.

Feeding a horse carrots, sugar, apples, or other delicacies is excellent practice if he receives such treats as a reward for good behavior in response to a signal or command. If you give him treats just for the pleasure of giving them to him, and not because he has earned them, you may find that he becomes ill-mannered or even resentful if you come around him without a love offering. He may show his resentment by laying his ears back or even nipping at other horses or kicking at them, and when a horse develops ill-mannered traits of this nature it does not add to his market value.

If you feed treats for a good cause they become an incentive to good behavior and this is laudable. But when you feed them be sure they are cut into pieces the right size for the horse to eat comfortably without choking on them.

Whenever you feed a horse anything from your hand, always extend the palm upward, with fingers turned down, never curled upward.

From this long list of safety precautions you may imagine that feeding a horse is pretty humdrum, possibly a tedious chore. But this is far from true. In fact, long-time horse owners will tell you that they look forward to feeding time with keenest pleasure. And you will discover yourself that some of the happiest moments of your life will be spent sitting quietly by, swinging your heels and nibbling on a straw, listening to your horse munch his dinner. Chomp, chomp, chomp — it's a rhythmic, restful sound, interwoven with the warmth of sunshine and the sweetness of hay and pungent horse scent; and it soothes away care and quiets troubled thought and establishes one of the most rewarding bonds known to horse lovers: the indescribable, tender benevolence that exists between the feeder and the fed.

6

Selecting His Wardrobe— and Other Appurtenances

OUTFITTING A NEW HORSE CAN BE AS MUCH FUN AS OUT-
fitting a new home or a new baby. You find yourself suddenly with an intense desire to adorn your four-footed
dependent with all sorts of high-fashion accessories which
will state clearly that he is well-loved, well-cared-for, and
well on the way to social success.

You can accomplish this quickly and without financial
embarrassment simply by shopping for essentials at first
and adding the niceties later.

The following items should head up your shopping list
since they will add to your safety and comfort as well as
the usefulness and elegance of your mount.

Equipment For Handling

TIE ROPES: At least three. (Two for cross tying, one for
leading or trailering.)

HALTERS: At least two. (One for everyday use and one for dress wear.)

LONGUE ROPE: One for exercising.

Equipment For Riding

HEADSTALLS: (Bridles and bits.) Preferably two, the style to be determined by the kind of riding you intend to do, whether English or Western.

TIE DOWNS: One of the type correct for your riding style.

SADDLES: (Including saddle accessories listed below.) One for the kind of riding your horse has been broken to, or a Western and English saddle if you intend to ride both ways.)

THE FOLLOWING ARE OPTIONAL:

    Saddle Pads
    Saddle Blankets
    Cooling Sheets and Blankets

Equipment For Grooming

Curry Combs (Metal and Rubber)
Cleaning Brush, Body Brush, Mane-and-Tail Comb
Scraper
Hoof Pick
Polishing Cloth
Electric Clippers (And kerosene with which to clean them)
Ribbons for braiding manes and tails

Health Aids

Dry Bran
Insect Repellant
Coat Conditioner
Hoof Oil
Tar Ointment
Gentian Violet

Vaseline
Sponges
Tranquilizers

Stable Equipment

Wheelbarrow
Pails
Pitchfork, Hay Fork, Blunt Shovel
Slaked Lime
Insect Spray
Shavings
Broom
Stable Boots, Gloves, Cutting Pliers, Hay Hooks

Equipment For Bad Weather

Waterproof Blanket
Pommel Slicker, Hat and Boots
Frost Nails for Icy Roads

Other Accessories

Special breaking and training equipment such as dumb jocks, breaking carts, pony harness, and bridles for colts, etc.

Special corrective equipment such as quarter boots, ankle boots, tail sets, etc.

If you plan to show or trailer your horse you will also want show halters, blankets, plastic feeding buckets and water pails, etc.

7
Playing Nurse

ON THE WHOLE HORSES ARE RUGGED ANIMALS, INCLINED TO be healthy. But certain nervous or high-bred horses may be inclined to intestinal disturbances or other minor ailments. It isn't good to neglect a horse that is obviously ill, but it is just as unwise to fret over your horse's health to the point where you encourage him to become a hypochondriac.

If a horse enjoys his feed and always eats all of it; if he has a gleam in his eye and a glow to his coat; if he does whatever is required of him with good will, you have no cause to worry about him. Just love him, enjoy him, and be grateful for his companionship.

If, on the other hand, a horse seems really dispirited; ignores his feed, fails to have regular bowel movements, or shows ill temper toward people or other horses, you should have a vet examine him. We do not recommend that you attempt to doctor a horse yourself for anything but very minor ailments. But since there will be occasions on which you may find yourself called upon to play nurse to your horse, we'd like to point out some of the more familiar symptoms of illness that you should watch for, and at the same time suggest ways of coping with them.

The Problem of Colic

The one ailment every horse owner should learn to recognize as quickly as possible is colic, a digestive disturbance caused by too coarse hay, spoiled hay, or an abrupt change of feeding habits. There are two kinds of colic, one much more serious than the other. Usually the condition results in a kinked or knotted intestine which prevents normal bowel movement. If the trouble is in the lower bowel an enema will usually relieve it. If it is in the upper intestinal tract it requires more drastic treatment which only a skilled veterinarian is capable of administering.

A horse with the colic usually stops eating, stops having bowel movements, appears restless and distressed, breaks out in a sweat, switches its tail, and sometimes lies down and snaps at its stomach.

As soon as you are convinced that a horse is suffering from colic you should call a vet and follow his instructions until he arrives. In all probability he will tell you to keep the horse on its feet and moving and not allow it to lie down till he gets there.

This may sound easy to do, but it isn't. A horse with colic is in such distress that he very much wants to lie down. But he must be kept on his feet and moving no matter how inconvenient this may be for his owner. And it can prove mighty inconvenient, especially if colic symptoms develop late at night when the temperature is nosing to zero.

Horses, like babies, frequently develop colic just when you're about to retire to your snug bed or take off for a social event, and it isn't exactly pure pleasure to be compelled to "walk the floor" with them.

However, it must be done. And chances are you will find that neighboring horse lovers, seeing the lights in your stable area at a time when they shouldn't be on, will suspect what is wrong and come over to help you with your vigil. This is the test of true friendship and results in a wonderful warm camaraderie as well as the rich reward of saving the life of a well-loved and valuable animal.

If you are called upon to administer an enema to a horse, on your vet's instructions (and never do so otherwise), be not dismayed. Use a small garden hose, covering the end (without metal attachment, of course) lavishly with vaseline; make sure tap water is at moderate temperature. Give the horse two or three quarts of the water through the rectum, then keep him walking until the enema takes effect.

Worms and Other Minor Maladies

Next to colic worms are one of the most frequent causes of discomfort and poor health in horses. And all horses, young and old, should be wormed at regular intervals if you hope to keep them in top condition.

If worms show up in a horse's droppings or if a horse eats constantly and still remains thin and gaunt, you should have your vet worm him. Don't undertake the job yourself. The worming seems simple to the inexperienced but it is a job which requires a vet's expert know-how.

You will find that worming a horse does almost as much for his appearance and temperament as having his teeth floated. It peps up his appetite so that he gets more good from his food and when he feels better he naturally becomes a more interesting friend and a safer riding companion.

Cuts and Bruises

We won't discuss any serious horse ailments in this section since it is meant only to tell you "what to do till the doctor gets there." For anything of a serious nature you should always consult a vet. But at the same time since vets are very busy people and frequently have to travel long distances to reach you, you should know what to do in small emergencies. And, under this heading, you will find at the top of the list, wire cuts.

Horses are like children in many ways. They're always getting into something: partly from playfulness and curiosity, partly from boredom. They stick their legs through fences and poke their heads through gates and between stall partitions where you wouldn't believe it possible for a cat to enter, and if there's any barbed wire within a mile of them they'll find it and, chances are, manage to become entangled in it.

If a wire cut doesn't require stitching, just rinse it out with tincture of green soap and water and daub it with Gentian Violet, the horseman's panacea. Watch to see how it heals and if it looks clean, all is well. If flies are prevalent, keep it coated with tar ointment. If any trouble develops of course call your vet.

Nail Wounds

If a horse gets a nail in his foot, extract it as soon as you discover it (and always inspect his feet daily for signs of nails) and have the vet give him a Tetanus shot. Clean the wound, soaking the hoof in Epsom Salts to keep it open and draining. (Special boots come for this purpose that tie around the horse's ankle and make soaking easier.)

Brittle Hooves

If a horse's feet seem to be hard and brittle, which is frequently the case in the drier portions of the South and West, make a depression in which he can stand and soak his feet. You'll need a pit about six inches deep and long enough for the horse to stand in, boarded and cemented at the base and sides so that it will retain water. Keep water running in this enclosure till the earth becomes muddy and have the horse stand in the mud at least an hour a day till his feet soften up. Repeat the process if his feet become dry and hard again at any time and in between soaking, coat his feet, including the frog, with hoof conditioner.

Lameness

Horses sometimes kick each other or knock their legs against stall partitions or fence posts, causing lameness. Unless the injury is serious you will find the lameness disappears if you run water from a garden hose on the injured area. Apply the water in a slow stream, for about 30 minutes at a time, at least twice a day. You won't mind the time spent in this manner because it will permit you to establish a beautiful, wordless affinity with your horse and at the same time it will help you to indulge in restful meditation which you might otherwise not have time for.

For slight sprains a good standby is Absorbine Sr. rubbed into the tender area.

To avoid injuries from kicking you should note if your horse is inclined to be kicky. If he is exceptionally so, even when mounted, you should ride him with a red bow tied to his tail if he is traveling with a group of horses. This tells other riders to stay clear of his heels.

If a horse receives an injury that takes hair off his hide, apply vaseline to the hairless area at least once a day. This will encourage regrowth of the hair and prevent scarring.

One safety measure you should always take to prevent injury to your horse is to remove his halter before you turn him out to pasture or turn him loose in his stall. Horses have a habit of scratching an ear with a back hoof and if the halter is left on they may become tangled in the halter, panic, and hurt themselves by running headlong into something.

Eye Troubles

If your horse's eyes water profusely or become reddened it may be because flies are bothering him or he has hay chaff or pollen in his eyes. Wash his eyes with cotton dipped in mild boric acid solution and if the soreness persists, apply ophthalmic ointment till they heal.

Skin Rash

If your horse continuously bites at himself or if his skin breaks out in a rash it may be that his feed is too rich and you will want to reduce the amount of protein in his diet.

These simple remedies and precautions should take care of most minor horse-ailments. But if at any time the symptoms of trouble seem too serious for home-style doctoring, we repeat:

DON'T FORGET !

CALL YOUR VET !

8
Beauty Care

THERE IS NOTHING THAT A GENUINE HORSE LOVER LOVES more than giving his horse a beauty treatment. And to look his best the well-loved horse should be given a thorough grooming every day. (Or at least immediately before you plan to ride him, if your schedule of duties is such that you can't afford time for daily beauty care.)

The correct steps to take are, first, to put a halter on him, attach a tie rope to the halter, and then cross tie him. Now take a rubber or metal curry comb and a brush and go over him entirely on one side, working from his head to his tail, using the curry comb to dislodge dirt and the brush to brush it away. And every few strokes, work the brush against the curry comb to remove loose hair.

If your horse is kept blanketed because you plan to enter him in shows, he won't grow as long a coat of hair as a horse left unblanketed or turned out at pasture.

But horses grow longer coats in winter and shed them in the spring, so there is always plenty of loose hair to

The most important safety measure you can take in working around or saddling a horse is to cross tie him properly. Fasten tie ropes to either side of his halter, then fasten to posts with slip knots.

This is a slip knot. One end remains free so you can pull the rope loose in an emergency. A horse should always be tied with this kind of knot.

remove in the grooming process. When working around his head remember that he can easily be made head shy if you use sudden or rough movements in grooming this area and his ears and his muzzle are especially sensitive, so never use a rough curry comb around those portions of his head. Instead use a polishing cloth or a soft brush. A horse never likes you to bend his ears or handle them roughly and he has such acute hearing that all sounds are intensely magnified close to his ear, so you must be mindful of this.

You should always tie a horse so that the rope can be pulled loose immediately if he starts to pull back. If a horse really pulls back hard he can injure his back legs seriously so always try to think ahead of him and have ropes maneuverable.

Wipe out his eyes and his nostrils with a clean damp cloth; brush his legs last, working downward and using a very gentle pressure because his legs are also sensitive and he may kick if the brush hurts.

Always stand to one side of the horse and out of range of his back feet if he is at all kicky. Never stand directly in front of a horse because he may throw out a front foot or rear up and hit you with his front feet. Never stand directly behind him because he may not see you clearly and may kick at you because he doesn't recognize you. If a horse kicks at you and you are to one side of him you will get less of the brunt of the blow than if you are directly behind him.

If you watch a horse closely as you groom him you will learn to see his muscles flexing or contracting and you will know if he is getting ready to kick. If he stands on three feet, with one resting, you can be reasonably certain that he isn't about to kick at you.

After you brush the loose hair off both sides and have

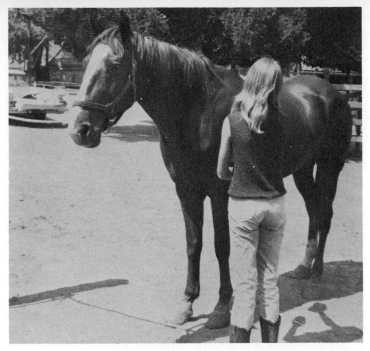

In grooming stand to one side, facing the rear of the horse and keep well out of the way of stomping hooves. Do not wear tennis shoes, open-toed sandals, or beach walks. Wear boots.

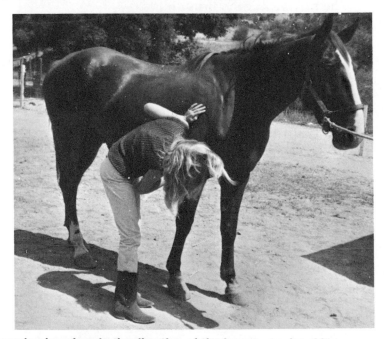

In grooming legs face in the direction of the leg you are brushing. Use a brush, not a curry comb, and brush firmly so as not to be mistaken for a tickle, which may cause the horse to kick.

Remove one tie rope when you work around your horse's head. Be gentle and approach his head slowly or you may cause him to become head shy, a dangerous vice.

loosed all the dandruff and dust from his hide you are ready to vacuum him, if you have a horse vacuum suitable for the purpose and he is accustomed to the sound of it; or you are ready to polish him with a clean dry cloth, preferably one made of wool. (Slick cloths or those made of synthetic fabrics won't work well.)

Then you comb his mane and foretop gently, holding the hair with one hand and working carefully from the bottom up to avoid tangling or pulls.

When combing mane and forelock stand to one side, not directly in front of horse where he could strike at you with his front hooves. And don't yank at tangles; disengage them carefully.

Hold the horse's tail first to one side, then the other, as you comb, working up from the bottom. Keep out of reach of kicks and be sure the horse is aware of you.

Next comb his tail, taking care to stand to one side as you do, and again work up from the bottom, gently, a strand at a time, to eliminate snarling.

A horse that is turned out at pasture may get nettles, burrs, and twigs entangled in his tail and may even get the tail so twisted up that you can't save it. To avoid this you should bring him in at least once a week and comb his tail so that he will not be shorn of one of his greatest beauty assets.

If you see tiny light specks on the ends of the hair on your horse's legs they may be the eggs of bott flies. To remove them, scrape them off gently with a single-edge razor blade or wipe them with a rag wrung out of kerosene. If a horse should swallow bott eggs they lodge in his stomach and eventually produce bott worms which cause severe disturbances in his digestive tract.

If the ground is muddy or your horse has been standing in manure you should clean his feet out with a hoof pick and then oil his hooves with hoof conditioner referred to earlier.

Occasionally a horse's mane will need to be clipped, his tail shortened, or his legs trimmed — depending on his breed, the way you intend to ride him, or the type of shows in which you plan to enter him.

If a horse is not accustomed to clippers he may require a twitch in his nose to make him manageable or you may have to stand him in a special enclosure while he is being clipped so that he can't strike at you with his front feet or kick at you with his hind feet during clipping. Only someone experienced in handling horses should be trusted to work around the hooves and heels of a green horse. Clippers make quite a loud noise, which is magnified many times by the sensitive ears of a horse; so it would be extremely hazardous to attempt to clip the ears or head of

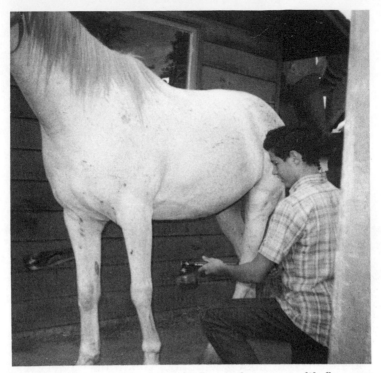

Before working around a horse in fly weather spray with fly spray. Apply sparingly; do not use spray gun on horse's head as it may make him head shy. Apply to head with cloth, lightly.

a horse not used to this sound. And after clipping it is good to clean the clipper blades in kerosene to remove hair and dirt and to prevent rusting.

In good weather you may want to hose your horse down but you must be certain that he is not sweated up before turning cool water on him. He should be cross-tied when you hose him and after he is thoroughly wet you use a scraper to run the excess water off. Then walk him till he is fairly dry and cover him with a cooling sheet. (If you turn him loose damp he will almost certainly roll in the dust.)

If the weather is hot and flies are a nuisance you should

spray your horse with insect repellant, taking care not to get the spray in his eyes or on areas which will be covered by the saddle or saddle pad. Spraying a horse against flies is a safety measure for you as well as comfort insurance for him because it keeps him from stomping while you saddle and mount him.

As you become wise in the ways of grooming your horse you will find it is a pleasure and not a chore because it gives you so much personal satisfaction to see him looking his best. Your horse also will look forward to the time that you spend on his beauty care since there is nothing more conducive to a feeling of self-respect on his part. A well-cared-for horse, sleek, shining, trim, and neat as any high fashion model says nice things about his owner with every prancing step and amply rewards you for the time and effort it takes to keep him beautiful.

9
When You Finally
Get To Ride Him

YOU HAVE COME A LONG WAY SINCE YOU DECIDED TO PUR-
chase a horse. You have selected the horse that is just right
for you; you've furnished a home for him, catered to his
taste in food, outfitted him in high style, groomed him to
sleekness and beauty, attended to his minor hurts, lavished
him with loving kindness, studied his disposition and character — now comes the glorious moment when you finally
ride him!

Or do you?

Not just yet. First you must learn how to saddle and
bridle him properly; how to mount him with grace and
how to handle him safely under rein.

To begin you must tie him correctly.

Be sure that he wears a halter then slip the clip of the
tie rope into the ring of the halter and fasten it to a solidly

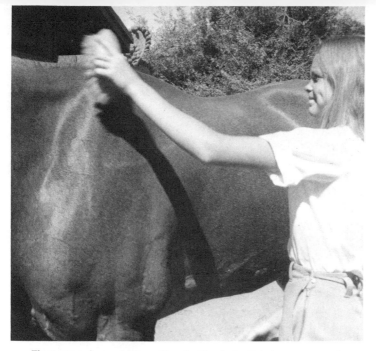

First step in saddling. Brush the hair flat to remove dust and to prevent saddle sores.

The English rider places a saddle pad or folded towel on the horse's back before saddling as a precaution against saddle sores.

The horse is made aware of the saddle before it is lifted to his back; then it is lowered gently in place.

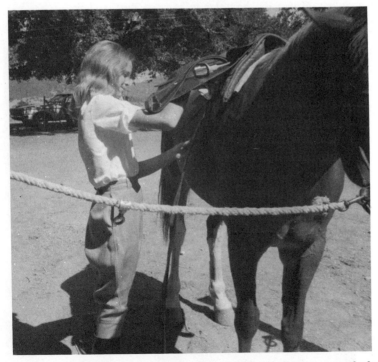

The rider now goes to the off side of the horse and checks to see that the girth is not twisted and that the stirrup is hanging properly. Look under the flap to be sure.

Having checked the saddle on the off side of the horse, the rider returns to the near side and lifts the flap, tightening the girth.

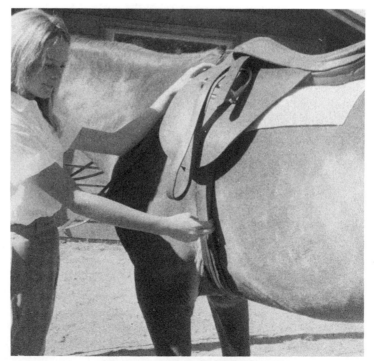

After tightening the girth moderately, walk the horse in a circle so he will relax, then tighten the girth a second time. You should be able to run your finger under it when it is just right.

Remove the halter and slip it around the horse's neck and fasten it there before you attempt to bridle him. In this way you have a means of retaining control of the horse if he should pull away from you as you start to bridle him.

First step in bridling: Hold top of halter in right hand and press down on horse's head. Slip thumb in horse's mouth so he will open it and accept the bit.

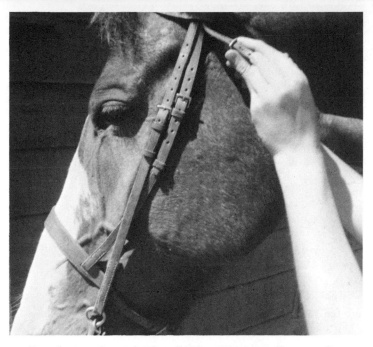

Now fasten throat latch, allowing room to slip your finger under it so it won't shut off the horse's wind if he flexes his neck.

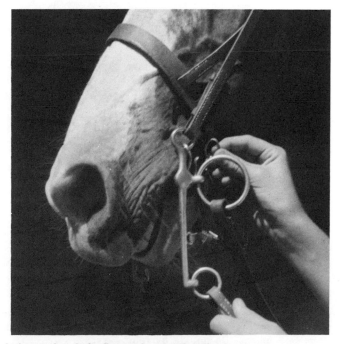

Fasten the curb chain so that it is flat and smooth, allowing room for you to slip a finger under it. Never fasten too tightly.

If you are too short to bridle your horse as just shown, open bridle at top, slip bit into horse's mouth, then refasten bridle.

To tie a horse that is saddled and bridled, slip reins behind stirrups and tie horse with tie rope, making a slip knot. Do not tie to flimsy fences. Do not tie by reins—ever.

If your horse hasn't been exercised recently lunge him in a circle at the end of a lunge line before mounting. Do this at least ten minutes in each direction. This is the most important safety measure you can practice.

To mount English style from the ground hold reins in left hand without pulling on horse; face rear of horse. Insert left foot in stirrup, which you hold in right hand. Spring from ground off right foot.

Next step in mounting shows rider retaining control of reins as she balances with her left foot in the stirrup and her right hand resting on the back of the saddle.

Retaining control of reins, throw your leg over the horse's back without touching it and drop lightly into the saddle. Engage off stirrup with right foot.

Observe the safety precaution of making your horse stand quietly for at least two or three minutes after mounting before allowing him to move off.

anchored object, preferably a post set in concrete. The rope must be tied so that it can be jerked loose instantly should he become frightened and pull back, otherwise he may pull so hard that he will injure his hind tendons and the rope will become so badly knotted that you will have to cut him loose.

Next brush the hair flat on his back, removing any dust that may cause irritation if allowed to remain under the saddle.

Now put the saddle pad or blanket on, letting him look

at and sniff it so that he will know what's going on and
not get snorty in the midst of saddling.

The saddle is brought to his attention after the blanket
has been smoothed and adjusted to the proper position
on his back. After he acknowledges the presence of the
saddle with a glance or a sniff it is put on his back in one
smooth, continuous movement and brought to rest on his
back *lightly*.

You have been working from the near (left hand side

**To dismount, place left hand on horse's neck in front of saddle;
swing right leg over horse's back without touching it and, grasping
back of saddle in right hand, remove left foot from stirrup.**

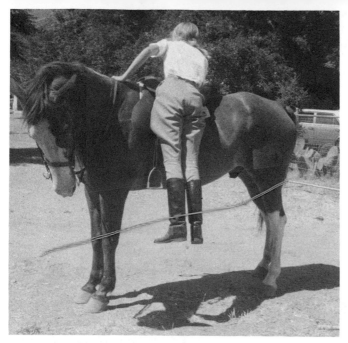

Continuing the dismounting action from previous photo, the rider is now in a position to drop lightly to the ground, retaining control of the reins.

Before removing English saddle slide stirrup irons up, unfasten girth, go to far side of horse, and fling girth across top of saddle. Now you won't trip over loose parts of saddle.

If you are too short to mount safely from the ground, use a mounting block. Accustom horse to block before trying to mount.

Let your horse eat at the mounting block. This is one way to make sure he will stand quietly to let you mount from it.

If weather is suitable hose horse's back under saddle after riding to remove dirt and sweat. If he is shy of a hose use a damp sponge. Keep hold of him but do not tie him.

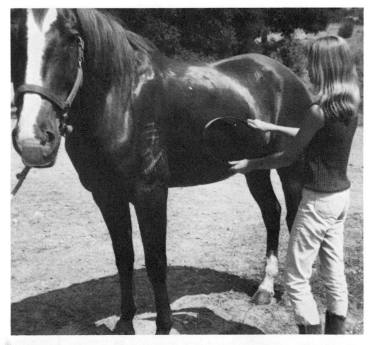

To remove excess water after hosing use a scraper. Stand well to one side, face horse's head, and curving scraper, pull toward you, working from top to under belly.

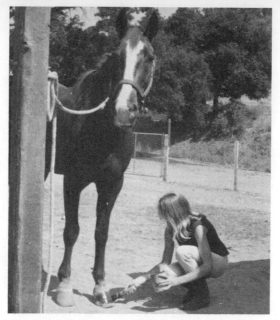

After riding, groom hooves with conditioner to avoid cracking and drying. Let horse see what you want to do and stay to one side well out of reach of pawing or stomping. Apply below hairline.

To catch your horse for mounting coax him with feed. If he's rope shy, keep rope hidden behind your back. Feed with palm extended flat.

Correct method of mounting bareback. Keep reins under control in left hand and vault lightly to the horse's back from the ground.

Correct seat bareback. Grip with knees, keep legs well forward. Never sink heels in horse's flank. If you do, you'll have a runaway.

of the horse facing his head) up to now, but at this point you should walk around to the other side of the horse to inspect the saddle to make sure that the blanket hasn't become displaced or curled up and to see that the stirrups or girth aren't caught under the saddle. It's a good idea to fasten the girth loosely at this stage because if the horse should give a leap before the saddle were fastened it might fall from his back causing him to be afraid of saddling from then on.

If everything is in place you are ready to tighten the girth.

Some horses may snap or pretend to snap at you when you go to tighten the girth simply because they don't like the feeling of discomfort that the girth gives them; or because a former owner has pulled the girth too tight in the past. Be prepared for a reaction of some sort by standing facing the horse and slightly away from him out of range of nips or kicks.

Don't slap at the horse if he registers a protest; simply speak firmly to him and shove his head away from you gently, until he learns to overcome his resistance to having the girth tightened.

No horse actually enjoys being girthed up; this is quite understandable since he feels the way you would if someone pulled your belt too tight without asking permission. Because he dislikes having the girth pulled tight he will probably blow up when you go to tighten it, especially if you're at all timid about dealing with him. Don't try to tighten the girth to the last hole all at once. Tighten it to the first hole and then bridle the horse before attempting to tighten it further. After bridling you can take it up another hole while his mind is on the bit in his mouth. Then walk him around a few times and you can probably sneak it up another hole just before mounting.

Correct way of leading horse. Hold lead rope in right hand close to halter. Gather ends neatly in left hand, walk abreast of horse, and use weight as leverage against his shoulder.

Cross tie properly, fastening tie ropes to halter, then to solid posts with slip knots as previously shown.

Inspect and clean horse's hoofs with hoof pick before mounting
to remove stones or mud. Photo shows correct method of working
with front hoof.

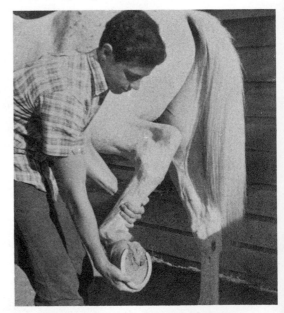

This is correct method of handling rear hoof. Stand facing rear
and close to horse so he does not have room to extend his leg
in a kick.

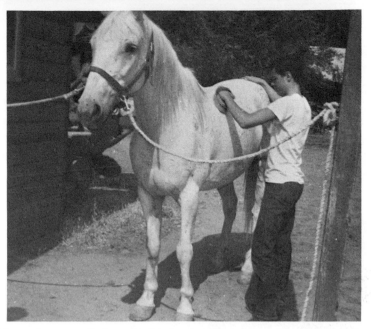

Properly cross tied and with hoofs clean, horse is ready for the next step in saddling. Now wipe off his back to remove dust and to straighten hair. This avoids saddle sores.

Now place saddle blanket evenly astride horse's back just behind withers in preparation for saddling in the western manner.

Allow the horse to see and sniff the saddle before you lift it to his back. Hook off stirrup over pommel.

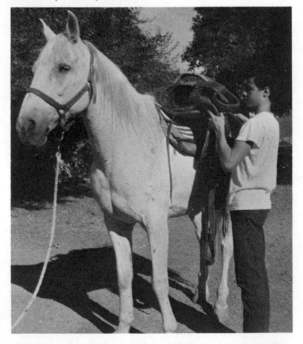

Moving quietly and with unhurried pace the saddle is now brought around to a position where you can lift it in place.

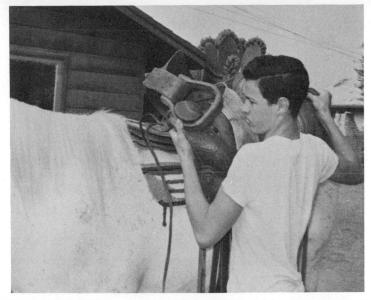

Lift the saddle high enough to avoid disturbing the saddle pad and then lower it gently to the horse's back.

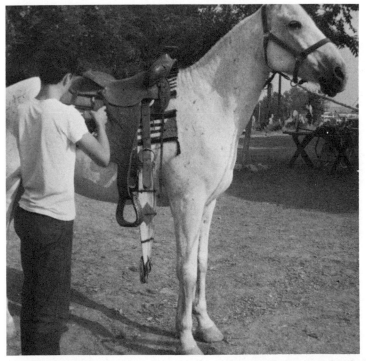

Now go around to the far side of your horse to make certain that nothing is caught under the saddle. Remove the stirrup from the pommel and gently lower it to the horse's side.

Tighten the cinch by pulling up on the latigo, but don't tighten completely at this point.

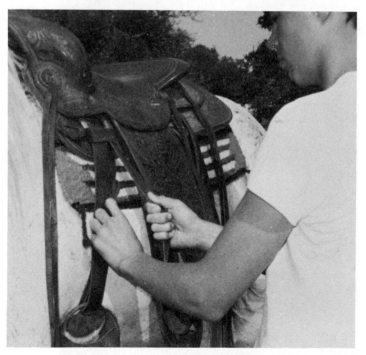

Walk the horse around till he relaxes, then complete the tightening of the cinch, leaving just enough room to slip a finger under it.

Lift the horse's foreleg to ease out any wrinkled skin that may be caught under the cinch.

First step in bridling: remove the cross tie ropes from the halter but do not remove halter completely. It provides a means for you to retain control of your horse as you bridle him. (See next photo for follow-through action.)

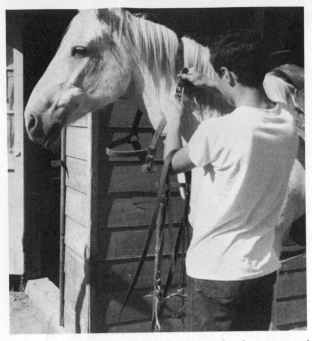

Halter is slipped back on the horse's neck and fastened there. Keeping hold of halter to retain control of horse, slide bridle down left arm and you are ready for next follow-through.

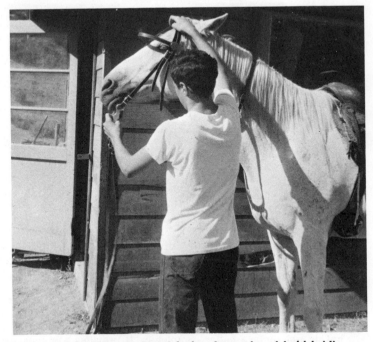

Allow reins to fall to ground. Stand facing forward and hold bridle at top in right hand. Lift bit to horse's mouth.

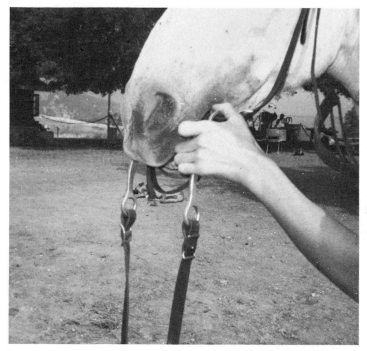

Encourage horse to accept the bit by inserting thumb in his mouth at the "bars"—the section of a horse's jaw where there are no teeth.

To bridle a horse safely you should take the bridle in your left hand and slip the halter off his head, keeping the tie rope fastened around his neck.

With the bridle in your left hand, slip the reins over his head and put your finger in his mouth at the toothless spot (bar) of his jaw and use the leverage your finger provides to pry open his jaw, at the same time introducing the bit into his mouth. If the horse is easy to bridle he will take the bit readily and you can then slip the bridle over his ears.

Look in his mouth to see that the bit is settled properly,

moving it back and forth lightly to be sure it is in place. Then fasten the throat latch, leaving at least a half inch of play in the strap so as not to cut off his wind when he flexes his neck.

Next fasten the chin strap so that it rests against his chin lightly. Do not draw tight.

If you are using a hackamore or bitless bridle you will find the bridling operation simpler since you merely slip the bridle over the horse's nose instead of maneuvering the bit into his mouth.

Now take the reins from over the horse's head, untie him and walk him around a minute or two, quietly. As soon as he is relaxed you can test the girth to see if it is tight enough. You should just be able to slip one finger under it.

Before mounting make a final inspection of saddle, bridle, and girth.

After completing your final inspection of saddle and bridle you are ready to mount the horse and you should master the safe way to do this.

Standing close to the horse and facing his tail, gather the reins in your left hand just tightly enough to keep the horse from nipping you in the back, should he feel so inclined, but not so tightly that you may cause him to back up. (You will be standing on the near side of the horse, which is his left side, facing him from the front. You always handle him, lead him, work with him, and mount him from this side, because except in rare instances the average saddle horse is broken to be approached from this side.)

Next put your left foot in the stirrup, turning the stirrup slightly so that it engages your toe readily, if you are mounting an English saddle; in the case of a Western saddle the stirrup will be in the right position to engage

Next fasten the throat latch making sure that you don't fasten it so tightly that it cuts off the horse's air supply. Run your fingers under it after fastening it. There should be room to move them about freely between the throat latch and his neck.

To complete bridling fasten chin strap, making sure it lies smooth and flat. Allow room to slip your finger under the chin strap after it is fastened.

If your horse is high headed or a head tosser attach tie down from bridle to girth as shown. The tie down always increases your control of the horse.

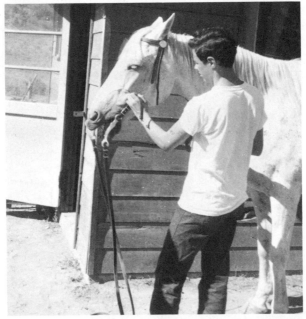

A rider who is not tall enough to bridle a horse comfortably may open the bridle as shown, insert bit in horse's mouth, and refasten bridle.

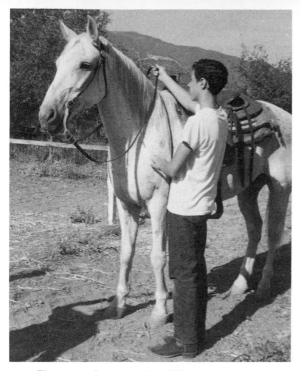

First step in mounting. Throw reins over horse's neck. If you are a beginner, you may wish to knot the reins so that you won't lose them.

Hold reins in left hand, grasp pommel with right hand, give a spring off your right foot and pull yourself up off the ground high enough to place your left foot in the stirrup.

Now throw the right leg over the horse's back without touching his rump.

Settle down lightly in saddle, placing right foot in off stirrup. See that horse remains standing before starting up. This is a safety habit that you should teach him.

Everything is wrong with this photo. Rider's hands and feet are not in proper position for mounting and—danger—a pet should never be allowed around a horse when you mount him.

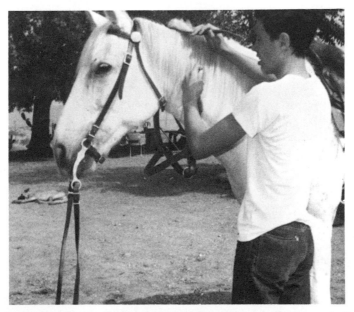

After dismounting, drop the reins to the ground and fasten a halter around the horse's neck before removing his bridle.

Slip bridle over horse's ears and ease it out of his mouth carefully. Snatching the bridle unnecessarily can injure the horse and make him difficult to bridle later.

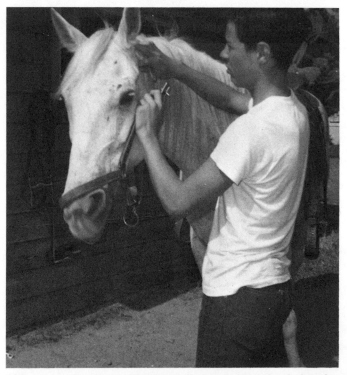

After removing the bridle immediately fasten the halter in place.

Cross tie your horse before removing his saddle. Slide saddle off in an easy sweeping motion, taking the saddle blanket with it. Allow saddle and pad to air.

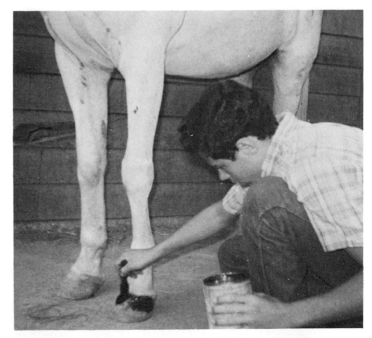

To keep hooves from drying and cracking brush with hoof conditioner after riding. Take safety position to right of horse, facing forward. Apply below hairline.

Correct method of releasing horse after riding: turn his rump away from you, unfasten lead rope, and quickly step out of reach of his hooves in case he wheels and kicks.

your toe. Now give a light spring off the right foot as you place your right hand on the saddle, lift your right leg up and over the saddle, easing yourself lightly down into the saddle as your right foot engages the right stirrup. (No kerplunks, please; they unsettle the horse by jarring his kidneys.)

See that the horse stands perfectly still for a few seconds after you mount him; don't let him take off immediately. The purpose of forming this good habit is to make certain that he won't move off too quickly and unbalance you before you have your "seat" in the saddle.

You should walk your horse a few minutes after mounting him — before extending to a faster gait, or before taking him off your premises — to be sure that he goes sound, hasn't any bucks in mind, and also to be sure that the saddle is tightly girthed after he relaxes. You can check the tightness of the girth by lifting one leg and one stirrup and slipping your fingers under the girth. With English tack you can usually adjust the girth without dismounting. With Western tack, if you find that the girth is too loose you will have to dismount to adjust it.

If you ride on public highways remember that in most states the rider is expected to keep to the right in the direction of traffic, not opposed to it.

At night the rider should always carry a flashlight or have reflectors attached to tack or tail.

Motorists are supposed to yield right of way to equestriennes but in this motorized age few realize this so don't depend on it. They should slow down and keep well away from horses who may shy at cars or at something else which causes them to land in the path of a car. If you are a horse lover we hope you extend these road courtesies to mounted riders, showing your understanding of horses in general and those on public highways in particular.

A horse should always be ridden on dirt rather than pavement if at all possible and he should never be galloped or even trotted on paved roads if it can be avoided since their shoes do not provide proper traction on such roads and they can easily slip and fall, injuring both horse and rider.

A horse should be put through all his gaits in the course of a ride but he should be allowed to extend to the gallop only while going away from home and should be ridden in controlled gaits when heading toward home. If he forms this habit and is compelled to stick with it you will never have a laggard on the way out and a runaway on the way home.

When riding with others the experienced rider always accommodates his gaits to that of the least experienced rider. And no courteous rider ever gallops off ahead of the group, because this is just inviting the other horses to take to their heels and follow.

A horse that has been used regularly gets muscled up to the point where he may be ridden fairly strenuously without prespiring profusely or getting sore. If your horse has not had sufficient exercise or has been eating hay alone without grain, he will be in a soft condition and should not be over-ridden; otherwise he may suffer serious discomfort if not injury.

A horse should not be galloped down hill or across rocky or gopher-ridden pastures for fear of stumbling. And he should never be galloped up steep grades or rugged terrain for obvious reasons.

A horse should always be allowed to become accustomed to any territory over which you expect to ride him while being ridden at a slow pace. This is because a horse taken away from home or ridden over strange territory for the first time may be extremely nervous and wary of every new object along the way.

If you are prepared for the possibility that your horse may shy or wheel at a strange sight or sound you will be less apt to lose your balance at his sudden movement and more apt to remain on top of the situation.

It is always a good idea to keep your mind on your horse. Pay attention to his muscles so you will know if he is tensing them for a sudden getaway; notice the way he rolls his eye or flicks his ears. These are all signals that prepare the experienced rider for the unexpected.

Horses react to things differently depending on the mood they happen to be in. One day a horse will move placidly along meadow or trail, giving you no cause for alarm. Another day, the same horse, going over the same ground, will shy at rocks or leafy shadows, at the stirring of birds or rabbits in the brush or at the sight of logs or puddles. You should be sensitive enough to your horse's moods to know what to expect from him.

If a horse once unseats his rider he has gained a point in his relationship to that rider and things will never be quite the same again. From then on he won't hesitate to see if he can gain a similar advantage. This is true of any form of misbehavior. If he outwits you one time he'll try for it next time and each time he succeeds you lose caste in his estimation. This is why it is so important to prevent trouble before it starts.

Reins should always be in hand, never slack. Knees should be kept tight, not flapping. Heels should be down, elbows in, back straight, attention concentrated on the horse, not on the scenery.

And, if you should be dismounted, recapture your horse and remount him at once.

The well-mannered rider makes a well-mannered horse, and such a horse is not permitted to nibble at grass or trees while he is being ridden; nor is he allowed to loll behind other horses, or stop at his own discretion. Once under tack a horse is expected to remain disciplined and under the control of his rider.

A horse should be walked the last half mile home and, if he is at all overheated you should walk him by leading him after you dismount. Remove his saddle first, putting it on a rack in the tack room or a similar place especially set aside for it; or if facilities don't provide such niceties,

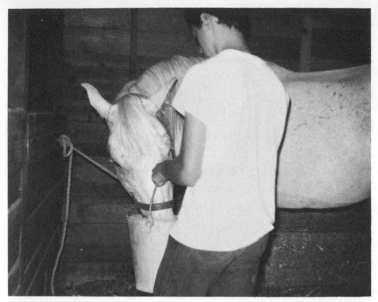

Before watering or feeding horse in his stall, tie him and approach him from the front. When you untie him step behind stall door as you turn him loose in case he kicks.

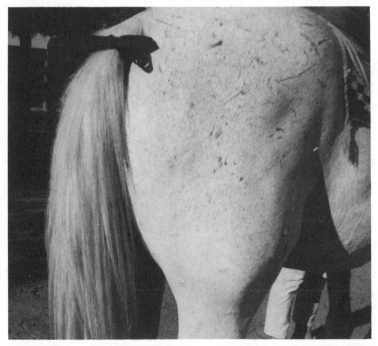

A red ribbon attached to the tail of a kicky horse tells other riders to keep their distance. This is a considerate safety precaution.

A horse can be aggressive at feeding time, especially around strangers. Take time to accustom your horse to your presence when he eats.

Regular inspection of tack is a good safety measure. And cleaning tack can be fun when your horse munches hay close by. He's not apt to be saddle shy after this treatment.

Play it safe at chore time. Tie your horse before you work around him in his corral or stall. Keep your mind on his heels and don't startle him.

A neat tack room is a safe one. Keep medicines and sprays neatly labeled and out of the reach of children. When saddles and bridles are hung up as shown you won't stumble over them.

place the saddle in a position where the tree will not be harmed. (The tree is the structure within the saddle that gives it shape and substance.)

Damp saddle pads should be aired and sunned before being used again.

The horse should be cross tied before his bridle is removed and one tie rope should be fastened to the halter which you put on him in place of his bridle.

Always rinse the bit in water after removing it and dry with a clean cloth; otherwise horse spittle or grass or other food which may have been in the horse's mouth when you bridled him will cake on the bit and become extremely difficult to remove.

Brush the horse or wipe him dry, being sure to straighten the hair under saddle and girth so it will be smooth when you wish to ride him again.

If you turn the horse out see illustration for correct method of removing the halter and rope, turning his rump completely away from you and keeping his head toward you so that he won't kick at you when he takes off.

Between ridings you should clean all leather tack with saddle soap and wipe clean with leather conditioner. Do this at least once a month — and oftener if you can manage the time — to keep all saddles, bridles, and halters supple and usable.

10
Going Places Together

RIDING YOUR HORSE ON YOUR OWN PROPERTY — IF YOU ARE fortunate enough to have riding room — or riding on equestrienne trails can be one of the most pleasant of life's experiences. But there will come a time when you wish to venture further afield: to shows or competitive horse events or just on visits to neighboring horse owners. When this time comes you will want a trailer so that you and your horse can go places together in style and in comfort.

You may not be able to buy a de luxe trailer at first but even if you start out with a home made model you'll love the freedom and adventure that trailering adds to horsemanship. Always select a trailer long enough, high enough, and wide enough for your horse; and be especially careful about sufficient headroom because if your horse konks his head the first time you try to coax him into a trailer you'll scarcely be able to blame him if he acts traumatic about trailering from then on. If you can't get a trailer with proper headroom it's better to get one open at the top although you will have to use more caution trailering a horse in an open-top trailer to protect him from drafts and cold. Certainly you will never want to trailer a perspiring horse in such a trailer and you will want to see that he is securely blanketed; possibly with protection for neck and ears — and particularly his chest.

A four-wheel trailer is easier to load and haul than a two wheeler even though it is certain to be more expensive. Other advantages which increase the cost but add to your pleasure and safety as well as that of your horse are: proper non-slipping matting on the floor and suitable drainage; an escape door at the front that you can come through when loading the horse; a dividing partition in a two-horse trailer, and most important of all, suitable wiring which allows for brake lights independent of your car braking system. (This set-up is compulsory in many states.)

Even a trailer-shy horse will eventually become accustomed to entering a trailer and even look forward to doing so if you let him eat his feed in it at least once a day over a period of two or three weeks.

Though the horse you buy may be accustomed to trailering he may not always step into a strange trailer without some hesitation. You will find it helpful to place some feed in the trailer and give him time to walk in after the feed the first time you load him. This method also helps to coax a horse into a trailer for the first time, especially if you are patient and allow him to look things over and don't try to hurry things.

Also, by keeping the trailer in plain sight and allowing a horse to graze near it, or by tying him to it regularly, it becomes familiar to him so that he loses his fear of it.

Horses sometimes have to be trailered to vets; or if you keep brood mares they must be trailered to the stud; also you may want to bring home a new horse in a trailer, or take him to the blacksmith if the smith can't come to you, so it's good sense to have any horse ready and willing to be trailered without resistance.

A horse that has had a bad experience in a trailer or one that has never entered a trailer before can give you a rough time if you try to load him hastily. If forced to enter a trailer against his will a horse will be doubly shy next time you try to load him.

Some horses may require a mild tranquilizer before loading. In any case it is wise to seek the help of an expert at loading horses if you are at all in doubt about the way your horse may behave. A horse may be coaxed or forced into a trailer but the instant he realizes he is inside it he may fly back out. This is the emergency for which you must be prepared with suitable rope arrangements. And someone must be present who is capable of closing the tailgate before he pulls back.

A trailer should accommodate grain, hay, a tub and bucket, a few drugs and grooming aids, and tack and gear.

You should never drive a trailer faster than state law permits, not only because you are law abiding and wouldn't wish to, but also because of consideration for your horse. A horse should be allowed to get out of a trailer and stretch his legs at least every hundred miles because the strain of keeping his balance within the trailer causes considerable tenseness in his muscles.

He should be fed and watered when you stop for food and you should always have a shovel and broom with you so that you can keep his quarters clean.

If you must stop at public places along the way you should arrange for reservations in advance, making certain that horses are welcome and that facilities are provided for trailers.

If a horse gets down in a trailer you must pull off the road as quickly as possible and try to get him on his feet again before he injures himself.

Be sure that your trailer is equipped with a fire extinguisher and see that the vehicle pulling the trailer has a suitable trailer hitch before attaching a trailer to it.

If you plan to take your horse to horse shows you will need to have entry fees paid in advance and you should also become familiar with show rulings regarding arrangements for stabling, feeding, exercising, and showing. When you arrive at the show you should go to the show manager or director and have trailer and stall space assigned to you. You will be required to pay board on a horse while he is at the show and you will want to pay for any special grooming or medical care that may be required. All gear, tack, and costumes worn during the show must meet the requirements of the show committee and agreements must be reached in advance of show time regarding which classes or events you wish to enter.

If you hope to be able to enjoy your horse both at home and away from home, now and in the future, there are certain things that you can do as a horse owner to insure this pleasure. You can do your part to see that suitable riding country and enjoyable riding trails are set aside now for the gratification of all future horse lovers.

The best way to do this is to join as many local and national riding clubs as you possibly can, take an active part in the plans of such clubs, and contribute your time as well as your money to seeing that suitable legislation is initiated and enacted to prevent the abolition of riding areas in your state.

If zoning follows the pattern it seems to be following today, particularly in heavily populated areas of the eastern seaboard and the southwest, there will not be sufficient

Loved since he was foaled, this youngster looks forward to being ridden.

areas left for the stabling of horses, much less for horseback riding. There are hundreds of thousands of horse owners in this country who can prevent this from happening if they will unite to see that their voice is heard.

Owning a horse is an enriching experience, extremely important to the character development of young people. Therefore the enjoyment of horses should be encouraged and every effort made to see that safe and beautiful riding trails are set aside now in communities throughout the country.

When two of your riding companions indulge in backyard gossip we hope they say nice things about you.

No true horse lover could contemplate the possibility of a world without horses. And it is unthinkable for those who love horses to imagine that pleasure riding may be prohibited in certain sections of our country simply for lack of foresight. You can show your regard for horses and your fellow horse lovers by making plans now to see that your local and national political leaders protect the interests of all horse owners through the enactment of proper zoning legislation today.

Index

117